Boost Your Employability

Sara Miller McCune founded SAGE Publishing in 1965 to support the dissemination of usable knowledge and educate a global community. SAGE publishes more than 1000 journals and over 800 new books each year, spanning a wide range of subject areas. Our growing selection of library products includes archives, data, case studies and video. SAGE remains majority owned by our founder and after her lifetime will become owned by a charitable trust that secures the company's continued independence.

Los Angeles | London | New Delhi | Singapore | Washington DC | Melbourne

SUPER
QUICK
SKILLS

Boost Your Employability

Felicity
Becker

Los Angeles | London | New Delhi
Singapore | Washington DC | Melbourne

Los Angeles | London | New Delhi
Singapore | Washington DC | Melbourne

SAGE Publications Ltd
1 Oliver's Yard
55 City Road
London EC1Y 1SP

SAGE Publications Inc.
2455 Teller Road
Thousand Oaks, California 91320

SAGE Publications India Pvt Ltd
B 1/I 1 Mohan Cooperative Industrial Area
Mathura Road
New Delhi 110 044

SAGE Publications Asia-Pacific Pte Ltd
3 Church Street
#10-04 Samsung Hub
Singapore 049483

Editor: Jai Seaman
Assistant editor: Lauren Jacobs
Production editor: Victoria Nicholas
Marketing manager: Catherine Slinn
Cover design: Shaun Mercier
Typeset by: C&M Digitals (P) Ltd, Chennai, India

Library of Congress Control Number: 2020941250

British Library Cataloguing in Publication data

A catalogue record for this book is available from the
British Library

ISBN 978-1-5297-4500-9 (pbk)

Contents

Everything in this book!

Section 1 How can I boost my employability?

Boost your employability by identifying what you are offering and what you want in return, creating a winning CV, and preparing for a successful interview.

Section 2 What career would suit me?

Don't get stuck in a rut! Recognize what you can offer the career market and what you want in return.

Section 3 Love it or loathe it?

A happy worker is a productive one. Make sure that you search for a job you will love and avoid the ones you would loathe.

Section 4 What skills are valuable?

Find out how much your skills are worth and what you should develop to get the career you want.

Section 5   How do I sell my attributes?

Establish what your attributes are and how to package them to target your ideal employer so that you stand out from the crowd.

Section 6   How do I make my experience count?

From informal qualifications to work history to life experiences: make it work for you.

Section 7   What is my brand?

Dust down your current brand (you will have one!) and cultivate it to boost your employability.

Section 8   How do I plan for success?

Thinking about how to plan effectively and who can help you will be important to your overall success. A good plan should have measures in place to keep you on track, so these also need to be factored in.

Section 9   How do I activate my plan?

Get your resources ready and your plan in action to get those checklists checked off. Find out how to manage bumps in the road.

Section 10   What are my next steps?

Do not lose your buzz or have a career slump. Keep up your great work on boosting your employability by planning your next steps.

...sting your employability is an excellent ...uit for a number of reasons. Firstly, ... are more likely to get your desired job. ...condly, it makes CV writing and inter- ...ws feel much easier. Thirdly, you should ...d it a rewarding and positive process that ...ves you confidence when applying for jobs ... promotions.

...When writing out your aims and objectives ...you should design them to be achievable, so ...keep the following in mind:

Ambition – think big

Intention – think about achievability and relevance

Mission – now focus it

Employability The things that make you employable such as skills, attributes, and experience. The presentation of this information about you is important to your overall success in becoming employed.

CV (Curriculum Vitae) A document outlining your attributes, skills, work experience, and achievements. This should be no longer than two A4 pages and should include your contact details. It is to be submitted to potential employers as a brief explanation of who you are and what you can do. Potential employers will decide whether to offer you an interview based on this.

Objectives These should be SMART and should all work together to achieve your overall aim. They can be small individual objectives or interconnected objectives, each relying on the completion of others. These can be short-term, mid-term or long-term.

How can I boost my employability?

10 second summary

Your employability will rely on you recognizing your skills, attributes, and experiences and then tailoring your CV and interview to match the expectations of potential employers.

60 se
summ

Take charge of your skills, attributes, and experiences

You may look around you at those who are in jobs that you really want to be in and wonder how they got there. You can get there too with a little bit of focus and energy. Whether you are just starting out, going for a promotion, or changing career path, boosting your employability can only do you and your career good.

Take charge of your skills, attributes, and experiences and harness them to work for you in achieving your ideal job. Once you have started, you will find it easier to recognize where you are going, what you want, and how you are going to get there.

Making your outcomes achievable!

To make easily achievable outcomes, follow these SMART rules:

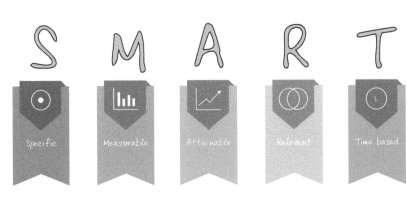

Specific – try to word your outcomes in specific terms, adding details that will help you to identify exactly what the task you need to achieve is. For example, if you are talking about painting a room, you would write what colour you are painting it.

Measurable – this usually requires a quantity here so that you can measure your outcome. Continuing with the room painting analogy, you would say that all four walls would be painted.

Attainable – this refers to how realistic your goal is. It would be no use to set yourself the task of painting a whole house, inside and out, without a ladder. You need to make sure that you have the resources and ability to achieve the desired outcome.

SMART This relates to the objectives you set yourself, which should be specific, measurable, attainable, relevant and time-based. An objective needs to be all these things so that you can achieve it.

Aim A broad view of what you would like to achieve. This could be short-term (a few days or weeks), mid-term (a few months) or long-term (a year or more). It should be broken down into and supported by SMART objectives. The aim is the overview of your objectives.

Relevant – this is particularly important if you are good at procrastinating as it can be tempting to set yourself irrelevant outcomes. If you are unsure if your planned outcome is relevant, try to think about how it will contribute to the success of your overall aim.

Time based – this is a very important element to prevent your actions taking longer than necessary. Set yourself a reasonable time frame in which to achieve the task, setting a review date or time to check that it has been achieved.

SMART outcomes

Have a look at the outcomes below as good examples and then have a go at writing your own SMART outcomes. For now, you are just practising this, so they do not have to be your final outcomes for boosting your employability.

Tip!

It is a good idea to put the time frame at the start, then it is easy to quickly scan your outcomes, see which deadline is closest, and focus your energy appropriately.

Examples:

By September this year, I will have applied for at least 15 jobs in marketing within a 20-mile radius of my address.

By July next year, I will have attended a networking event and have made 3 useful contacts, who I will be in touch with by the second week after the networking event.

....

....

....

....

....

....

What are my long-term, mid-term and short-term objectives?

Depending on your situation, your range of objectives may vary. If you are looking for a new job, your long-term objective may be getting that job, your mid-term objective could be creating a strong network around you, and your short-term objective might be to write your CV.

If you are seeking a promotion or advancement in the career you are already in, your long-term goal may be a job role two or three positions higher than your current one. This would be reflected in your mid-term objectives (which might be to get a promotion into the next job up) and your short-term objectives (boosting your work profile and taking on responsibilities in preparation for promotion).

Whatever your objectives are, try to only have a few at any one time.

Network This is a group of people who you can speak with about your career. A network can include relatives, friends, ex-colleagues, current colleagues, managers, teachers, academic supervisors, professional mentors, and people in the same field of work who might be able to help you.

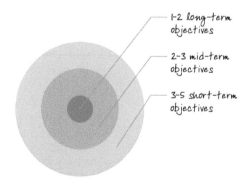

1-2 long-term objectives

2-3 mid-term objectives

3-5 short-term objectives

Is my current method of job searching working?

There are two things that can boost your job search:

1 Broadening your job search activities.
2 Improving the effectiveness of your covering letter/CV/application form.

If you believe that your method of job searching is not producing the results you're wanting, look to broaden your search by asking your network for advice, utilizing job advertisement websites, approaching your local job centre, checking out specific companies' websites, and so on.

If you are unsure which career to go into or whether you want a promotion, speak with someone you trust who knows you well. Make sure there is plenty of time for an in-depth discussion and be prepared by knowing what you want out of the conversation. You should choose someone who will challenge you if they think you are going down the wrong path, as it is sometimes easier for a third party to see the bigger picture.

How do I start?

Write out your aim and SMART outcomes and put them somewhere you will see them when you are thinking about, and working on, boosting your employability.

Your outcomes will change as you progress so you will update this document as you go along. Do not worry if you only begin with two to three outcomes; a slow and steady start is often the way to success.

CHECK POINT Make a start

Work through the following questions

What is my overall aim?

....

....

....

What are some of my SMART outcomes for short-term, mid-term, and long-term objectives?

....

....

....

....

....

....

....

....

....

Who will I talk with to get some advice about how to achieve my outcomes?

....

....

What career would suit me?

10 second summary

It is easy to get stuck in a rut. This is your chance to revaluate and to open your eyes to careers that you might not have thought of before.

Finding my perfect career

When starting out on your employment journey you are likely to have a narrow view of the career market. You may have thought, for example, that with an English degree you would be going into publishing, editing, journalism, teaching, and other similar careers. However, an English degree is also useful in marketing, media, theatre, management, training, and any job that requires professional, written English.

Looking beyond the obvious can be an exciting prospect and this section will get you started.

A student told us

'I've always known what my dream job would be.'

Dream job or fantasy?

Your 'dream job' is not always what you think it is, so take time to examine what will make you happy in a job. Your personality has a lot to do with your happiness and success in a workplace. Reflect on the jobs you have had; which parts of them made you feel energetic, happy, and secure?

Finding your work personality

Have a look at the four work types below and reflect on which one best matches your personality, and whether more than one could apply to you. (You should think of examples of your personality from both your personal and work life.)

- Logical, analytical, and data-orientated.
  - You like systems, you enjoy puzzles and problem-solving.
- Organised, plan-focused, and detail-orientated.
  - You will plan for most things and work out the details before you do tasks.
- Supportive, expressive, and emotionally orientated.
  - You like sharing your ideas and teamworking. You will use gut-instinct and check that everyone in the team is alright.

- Strategic, integrative, and idea-orientated.
  - You think about the overall picture, plan ahead, and know who would carry out each task best. You want everyone to get involved.

Once you have worked this out, it will be easier to know what types of jobs would suit you.

Tip!

Find out your personality type before applying for jobs to check that you are not going down the wrong path. There are plenty of personality tests online.

Utilizing your network

Your network is made up of friends and family, previous academic tutors, and acquaintances you have made through work experience, volunteer work or training courses. There are also professional networking events that you could attend to expand your network.

Work experience
This could be from paid or unpaid work and includes any experience in which you were responsible for performing tasks to achieve a set goal for the benefit of a work project or work team.

Chart your network

Look at the example, and then use the space below to chart your own network

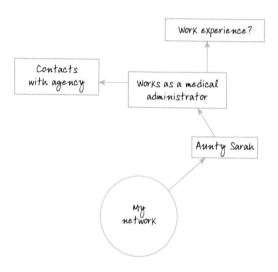

As referenced in the above quote, you should know what it is you have to offer others and begin building your network through generosity.

Getting a recommendation goes a long way. Your network will also help you to determine what you want to do, what a job really involves, and how to go about getting it.

The hidden job market

Not all jobs are advertised in such a way that you would find them. If you know your dream job is with a specific company, start off by checking their website for job opportunities. Even if they don't have anything for you there, contact the recruitment team (usually within the HR department) to ask them to keep your details on file and to find out if anything is likely to come up soon. Receptionists might be the keyholders to your ideal job as they often know what is coming up and they talk with everyone within a company, including the people who might interview you. Ask your contact within a company to keep your details on file for future job opportunities.

Hidden job market
This describes all the jobs that are not being advertised publicly but are being shown on individual company websites, internal to an organization or through word-of-mouth. For example, a manager may ask their team to put forward anyone they know who might be interested in the job vacancy. This is where your networking will be useful.

Tip!

Check in every 3-4 months so you can't be forgotten.

Which companies or organizations would suit me?

Think about what is important to you in a company. Ask yourself, is it:

- their ethical values?
- the additional benefits and perks they offer?
- the amount of holiday you would be entitled to each year?

Values These are the core things that you hold dear such as honesty, maintaining a work-life balance, family, and so on. If these differ from the values of the company you work for, you may find this a difficult situation to be in.

- the salary they pay in comparison with similar jobs in other companies?

- the flexibility of working hours?

- their vision?

Once you have listed what is important to you, you will find it easier to target the companies that will give you the sort of work life you want.

Resources to improve my success

You may want to use a careers service if you feel that you do not have enough time or energy to put into your job search. A careers service will offer to do personality tests with you, help you write a CV and covering letter, search for relevant jobs for you, fill in and send off applications on your behalf, and so on.

Other resources to consider

- personality tests

- CV templates

- covering letter templates

- lists of interview style questions

- companies' websites

- websites that offer a 'rate my workplace' function, such as www.glassdoor.co.uk (although be wary of disgruntled ex-employees using these)

- Office of National Statistics – for earnings and hours worked by industry (if you are trying to work out average salary)

- employment websites that advertise jobs

- www.gov.uk (for your employment rights and other information about tax and National Insurance)

CHECK POINT Preparing to target your job search

Work through the following checklist to narrow down your job search

What is my work personality?

....

....

....

....

Five jobs that would suit my personality:

1 ....

2 ....

3 ....

4 ....

5 ....

Who have I identified as being in my network?

....

....

....

....

....

Five companies that might have my perfect job:

1 ....

2 ....

3 ....

4 ....

5 ....

Which resources will be useful to me?

....

....

....

....

....

....

Which career type will suit me and my lifestyle?

....

....

....

....

....

....

Love it or loathe it?

10 second
summary

It is important that you decide what
you would love or loathe in your career
before you go any further.

60 second
summary

Learning what to keep and what to drop

Although you can learn to find value in most things, you are better off not wasting time in a job that will not help you achieve your career dreams. However, it can be hard to not fall into a convenient job, a job someone else thinks you would like, a job that pays the bills but nothing more. An ill-suited job can negatively impact on your mental health, which may lead to longer-term issues with your physical and emotional wellbeing. A job that suits you will complete you, not deplete you.

So, you need to work out what you can stand and what you will not stand for at this point.

What practical things would make me happy?

So that you do not get side-tracked into a job that will not satisfy you, take time to think about what is important to you in a job by completing the activities on the following page.

ACTIVITY The things that are important to me in a job

Set out your priorities. Tick those that apply to you and add any additional considerations below:

- ☐ flexible working hours
- ☐ health scheme
- ☐ medical insurance
- ☐ money – salary
- ☐ money – from bonuses or commission
- ☐ opportunities for promotion
- ☐ in-house training opportunities
- ☐ a strong team

Additional priorities:

....

....

....

....

....

Follow the step-by-step guide below to build a picture of what type of work activities would make you happy. Use the table on the following page to jot down your thoughts.

1   Thinking back through your life experiences (not just work), write a list of up to eight that have made you feel happy, satisfied, energized, or motivated.

2   For each one on the list, write two to three key parts of the experience that made you feel that way.

3   Check if there are words that keep coming up and make a list of them.

4   Thinking about the line of work you are looking to get into, will it satisfy the things on that list you have just made?

5   If yes, then you know you are on the right track. If not, then you may need to revise the type of job you are looking for.

6   Keep this exercise as it will help you to improve your CV.

Example

Experience	What made it great?
E.g. sky-diving in France	• being out of my comfort zone • the risk • being with new people
E.g. presenting at an academic conference	• being out of my comfort zone • meeting new people • talking and hearing about an area I'm interested in

Key considerations:

- risk/challenge
- meeting new people
- out of comfort zone: a back-office job will not satisfy me but a customer facing job with the opportunity to be involved in lots of new projects would

Experience	What made it great?
1	
2	
3	
4	
5	
6	
7	
8	

Decide whether you would be happy working with others or whether that would drain or frustrate you. Consider what working with others entails and then decide whether that appeals to you or not. Working with others could involve:

- negotiation

- sharing information (professional or personal)

- dealing with problems together

- communicating with colleagues regularly (and listening to them)

- motivating other people

- patience

- creativity

- empathy

- excellent interpersonal skills.

Consider what it would mean to work alone:

- necessary to self-motivate

- responsible for time and task management

- nobody to bounce ideas around with

- problem-solving alone

- flexibility in terms of how, where, and when you work

- nobody to get you out of a rut

Some people love working in an office with a team; other people love working outside. These are only two of the environments that might make you happy but think about this further to create a description of your ideal work environment.

A student told us

'I have only ever budgeted as a student. I'm not sure what other expenses might come up...'

Money matters

Although there is the well-rehearsed saying that 'money can't buy happiness', it can have a seriously detrimental impact on your happiness if you are worrying about how to pay your bills. By assessing what you need to live the lifestyle you want to live, you will be able to ascertain what income you will be satisfied with.

The table below should help you get started in planning the minimum income you would need. Feel free to add more items to the list:

Outgoing item	Current cost per month	Current cost per year	Will this go up in the next 5 years?
E.g. mortgage/ rent	£800	£9600	Yes
Mortgage/rent			
Bills			
Telephone			
Internet			
Car (petrol/tax/ insurance/ repayments)			
Food			
Clothes and other accessories			

Leisure			
National Insurance			
Life insurance			
Technology/ books/etc.			
Qualifications			
Children (clubs, etc.)			
Charities			
Savings and investments			

What should I get rid of now?

Now you have worked through this section, get ready to remove any jobs that fall into the following categories:

- A salary that does not meet your needs.

- Any job that has an element you cannot stand (e.g. working alone, travelling lots).

- A job that has no room for progression or development (unless you are already at the top!).

- Any jobs that do not aim you at your ideal future career.

You may add to the above list but this is a good place to start.

What should I NOT compromise on?

Your happiness. Ultimately, you will have created a priorities list that will (you think) make you happy. If a job comes along that ticks a lot of boxes but does not meet your top priorities, then you risk not being happy with it long-term. Consider a time in your life when you have had to do a task you did not want to do. Now think about how it made you feel. Sad? Angry? Frustrated? Stressed? All these feelings have the capability of affecting your hormones, which in turn influence your mental and physical wellbeing. If you were to do a job that made you feel these negative emotions on a daily or weekly basis, you are likely to suffer longer-term mental health problems. So now is the time to think carefully about what would have a negative impact on your happiness and wellbeing.

CHECK POINT Establishing my needs

Ask yourself...

What are my top priorities when searching for a job?

1 ....

2 ....

3 ....

4 ....

What makes me happy?

....

....

What are my total living costs?

....

....

Which jobs will I get rid of?

....

....

What will I not compromise on?

....

....

Tip!

It can be difficult to think of what you will and will not compromise on until you are in the workplace or have been offered alternative solutions. You will be clearer on this as you gain more work experience.

Congratulations

Now you know what career you are looking for. Write
it down here:

....

What skills are valuable?

10 second
summary

All skills are valuable depending on the circumstances. Now you know what type of employment you are seeking, select the skills that will match it.

Searching for skills to lead to success

You have limited time with a prospective employer and your first point of contact with them is through an application form, CV and possibly a covering letter. It is vital that you get your skills across quickly and effectively at this point to make it any further in the recruitment process.

Choosing which skills match your ideal job and then finding a way to demonstrate them is your best chance of reaching the interview stage. Once you are there, giving clear examples of your skills and the impact of them will raise your chances of securing that job.

Skills are what you have developed through training or experience, such as good accounting, professional writing, and customer communication skills.

What are my skills?

Complete a 360-degree review by writing down what you think your skills are and what other people think your skills are. Try to choose various people who have seen you in different scenarios: as their manager, as your superior, as your peer. This is a useful exercise as it will give you the full picture of your skills from other people's perspectives as well as your own. Quite often you will find that someone else has different ideas about your skills (or the extent of them) than you do, so involving others can be beneficial.

Skills These are things you have had to learn or develop, either formally or informally. They include project management, organizational skills, stress management, time management, communication skills, leadership skills, and flexibility. They could also include more job-specific areas such as accountancy, computer skills, teaching skills, and so on.

'Make the most of what you have got.'

How do I assess which skills are useful in my chosen career?

Look at job adverts and highlight every skill they refer to, such as 'accounting', 'proofreading experience', 'management'. You will then be able to get a clearer picture of what skills are required and you can review your own list considering this. Remove any skills you have that are not required in your chosen career from your CV master copy but keep your skills list in case you need it for future reference.

How do I prove my skills to potential employers?

You should already have a skills list, now you need to write two to three examples of when you have used these skills. (These experiences do not have to be purely professional ones as employers like to see you as a well-rounded person.) Put at least one example in your CV. Keep your other examples handy as preparation material pre-interview.

Attributes These are your personal qualities that can be polished but are unlikely to change dramatically. They are things such as honesty, personal presentation, positive attitude, reliability, self-management, enthusiasm, social responsibility, autonomy, and learning at work.

Tip!

When you have found examples of your experience with certain skills, attributes, and values, you should be able to pinpoint the examples that demonstrate at least two or all three and these are your best stories to share in interview.

A student
told us

Developing new skills

It is important to talk about your planned activities to develop your skills with someone so you can bounce ideas around. You will also be held to account by someone who has offered you some assistance, which will motivate you to continue.

There are the obvious ways to develop new skills such as courses (in-person and online), individual research, and tests. However, you may find other opportunities that suit you better. For example, you might shadow someone in their work, gain some work experience, or take on voluntary work. A lot of employers value hands-on experience as it means that the skills you are gaining are not simply theoretical or based on ideal conditions but are skills that have been put to the test.

If you are already in a job, you may seek out skills development within it. This is a particularly important step if you are boosting your employability for a promotion within the same line of work.

Even if you are still in the process of skills development when you submit your CV, include it but be clear that you are undertaking a course (or similar) and when you expect to finish it. Employers will be impressed by your proactive attitude towards developing your professional skills.

What if an interviewer asks me about a skill I do not have?

You should take this sort of a question as a positive sign – they are interested in you enough to ask the question. You may want to prepare an answer to this along the lines of 'that's an interesting point. I have wondered about how best to develop this skill. I'd be grateful for any guidance you could give me'. This way, you have shown willing, you have placed the interviewer firmly in the role of expert (which they are likely to enjoy), and you will hopefully receive some useful information. Alternatively, you could say that you are in the process of researching how best to develop this skill.

ACTIVITY Skills for success

What are my skills?

....

....

....

....

Examples of when I have demonstrated those skills:

....

....

....

....

Which skills do I need to develop?

....

....

....

How will I develop them?

....

....

....

CHECK POINT

Planning to answer tricky questions about skills

1. On several pieces of card, write out potential answers to tricky questions that interviewers might ask you in relation to skills you do not have or are still developing.

2. Ask someone to ask you the questions you might expect in your interview about these skills and use your cards to answer them.

3. Ask your 'interviewer' for feedback as to which ones seemed most natural and convincing.

4. Alter your answer cards if you need to.

How do I sell my attributes?

10 second summary

Your attributes are part of your personality. These are key to your employability as they will either make you well-suited or ill-suited to a job.

60 second
summary

Assessing my attributes

Everyone has their own set of attributes such as good time-keeping or excellent communication; these will be of interest to employers who want to find someone who has the right attributes to be successful in the job. You can only sell your attributes to potential employers if you know what they are, so taking the time now to identify your natural attributes will be worthwhile. Finding examples of when your attributes have been demonstrated will give your interviewers tangible evidence of how you have utilised them effectively. Skills and attributes often go hand-in-hand, so find out how to recognize your attributes and then how to use them effectively to win you your perfect job.

A student told us

What are attributes?

Skills are learnt, although your natural attributes might assist you in doing so. Your attributes could be called your 'natural skills', such as time-keeping, good communication, good work ethic, enthusiasm, problem-solving, and so on. These attributes will have been developed in your childhood and often support your values.

Graduate attributes are academic based, such as:

Graduate attributes
These are attributes that are usually associated with graduates as they tend to relate to academia. They might include intellectual curiosity, research presentation, critical thinking, problem solving, communication skills, creativity, and so on.

• intellectual curiosity

• respect for the values of your chosen profession

• respect for truth.

It is worth noting that if a job advertisement has talked about graduate attributes, they may also consider you if you are not a university graduate but have evidence of similar attributes. Graduate attributes are usually developed alongside your main course of study and universities often run schemes through which you can develop and demonstrate these attributes to boost your employability.

'Extracurricular, extra potential!'

How do attributes help me choose a career?

By this point you might have a clear idea about which industry you would like to go into and so you are narrowing down the job roles in this area. You should begin by writing down your attributes, perhaps finding help in recognizing them. Once you have done this, start ruling out jobs that do not match those attributes. For example, if you do not have 'working well under pressure' on your list, choosing a highly pressurized job with lots of deadlines would result in high levels of stress. If you have 'good communication skills' on your list, then a customer facing or collaborative job would suit you well.

Tip!

> Your attributes and your temperament will be better suited to some careers and not to others. Finding out what suits you early on will save you a lot of hassle.

How do I advertise these attributes?

Your first chance to do this is in your CV. Once you have selected three to five key attributes, find examples to back up your claim to them; these should be from your professional or educational experience, if possible, but you can also dip into your personal life for examples. Your second opportunity is at interview. Be ready with further examples of other attributes you have. Your attributes will be woven into your CV in the 'personal profile' and 'skills' sections.

Are there any attributes I should avoid mentioning?

When writing your CV it can be tempting to include the attributes of which you are most proud. Try to be practical and limit it to those that will get you the job. Struggling to do this? Write out all of your attributes and match them to those found in job adverts that interest you. This will give you a clear idea about what you should and should not mention. In consolation, it may be that at the interview you will have an opportunity to mention your other attributes.

If your attributes do not match those required by a job, this might be the time to reflect on whether you have chosen a career that will truly suit you.

Do not forget that within any one industry there are many, many job roles and they all require something different.

How do I stand out from the crowd?

This is the bit that can seem tricky but is fairly simple when you get started. To stand out from the crowd you need to blend your attributes in with your skills to make it clear that your natural talent for something supports your learnt skill. In an interview, you should aim to use examples of your skills that also highlight your attributes. This is something that gets easier with practice.

CHECK POINT — Blending your skills and attributes

Have a go at highlighting the skills and attributes in different colours below.

> I first learnt how to produce online presentation materials through my university's graduate development scheme. I worked with a small team to follow the instructions and then problem-solve in order to create materials using the best software available to us. My own experience of watching presenters at conferences helped me to think about what would work well and what wouldn't be effective.

The above example shows off skills and attributes seamlessly. Now have a go at writing two to three paragraphs combining your skills and attributes.

....

....

....

....

....

....

....

....

....

....

Answer

(Skills are written in yellow, attributes are written in green.)

I first learnt how to produce online presentation materials through my university's graduate development scheme. I worked with a small team to follow the instructions and then problem-solve in order to create materials using the best software available to us. My own experience of watching presenters at conferences helped me to think about what would work well and what wouldn't be effective.

Example

The skills demonstrated here are:

- production of presentation materials

- small teamwork

- using presentation software.

The attributes demonstrated here are:

- a proactive nature evidenced through being part of the graduate development scheme

- problem-solving

- communication and negotiation is implied through problem-solving as a small team

- intellectual curiosity as seen by their attendance at conferences and the reflective practice undertaken following conferences.

ACTIVITY

Identifying and evidencing my attributes

What are my top five attributes?

1 ....

2 ....

3 ....

4 ....

5 ....

What do employers in my sector want?

....

....

....

....

....

....

....

....

....

....

....

I have two to three examples of my attributes in action:

....

....

....

....

....

....

....

....

....

....

What I will say in an interview about my attributes:

....

....

....

....

....

....

....

....

....

How do I make my experience count?

10 second summary

Whether you have a lot of work experience or no work experience, it is important to know how to package it. The volume of experience matters less if it is presented correctly.

Super-charging my CV

A potential employer may not take the time to read between the lines to discern how much work experience you have had or how relevant it is to the role for which you are applying. It is your responsibility to make employing you seem the easiest and most obvious decision and the more evidence you put forward that you are the perfect candidate, the better.

Take the time to learn how to package your experiences to be the most appealing to potential employers and boost your employability. Once you have started to do this, it will begin to feel much easier to continue.

Does 'experience' mean 'work experience' only?

If an application form asks specifically for 'work' experience, then you can only refer to paid and voluntary work experience. If an interviewer asks you to share any of your experiences that would prove you have specific skills or attributes, you may draw on both work and personal experiences. On your CV, you should have a section detailing your work history, so that will be covered. Take the opportunity under the other sections to share details of personal experiences that demonstrate your skills and attributes if you have limited work experience.

If you are just starting out on your career journey, make it clear to employers why you have little or no work experience. Make sure that you cast it in the best light by saying something along the lines of 'I have spent the past three years focused on achieving my undergraduate degree in...' or 'I have spent the past ten years focused on raising a family....'. Employers will feel relieved to know why you have limited experience. You should quickly follow it up with a detailed account of the skills you have learnt outside of work.

What skills might I have from my non-work experience?

In the middle of a blank piece of paper, write the reason you do not have work experience. (For example, 'parenthood' or 'studying'.)

From that central point, draw lines out and write down the skills you have used in your daily life. See two real-life examples below.

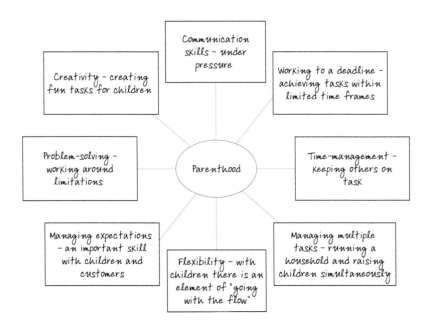

Communication skills – under pressure

Creativity – creating fun tasks for children

Working to a deadline – achieving tasks within limited time frames

Problem-solving – working around limitations

Parenthood

Time-management – keeping others on task

Managing expectations – an important skill with children and customers

Flexibility – with children there is an element of "going with the flow"

Managing multiple tasks – running a household and raising children simultaneously

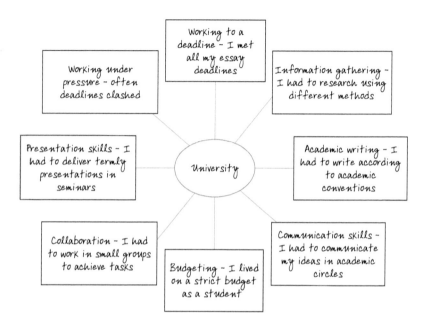

Once you have created this spider diagram you will have a clearer idea about what to include on your CV and what you should refer to if the opportunity arises during an interview.

What are employers looking for from my experience?

Sometimes employers are looking for someone with a wealth of experience. Sometimes employers are looking for someone with little experience so that they have the chance to train them up in-house. If your dream job arises but they require more experience than you have, do not be disheartened; look back through your spider diagram and see if you have gathered that experience in different ways.

How can I get more work experience?

You could get additional work experience by doing any of the following:

- Applying for voluntary positions.

- Asking a local business if you can join them for work experience for a short period of time.

- Checking out apprenticeship schemes.

- Asking your network to see if anyone can offer you a work experience opportunity.

Tip!

Avoid spending too long in unpaid positions. If you are no longer getting anything useful from it, then move on to something new.

- Unpaid experience can potentially become a paid job.

- Receiving training.

- Building your network.

- Devleoping informal skills.

- Appreciating what the job entails.

Consider what you would get out of an unpaid placement. Your uptake of numerous work experience opportunities will show potential employers that you are proactive and energetic where your career is concerned. When thinking about taking on unpaid work, you absolutely must consider the financial impact this will have on you though. If you are in a position where you are able to financially support yourself whilst doing volunteer work, then that is fine. However, if volunteering will mean you will suffer due to a lack of funds, then you should only be searching for paid work. It may be that you can find a balance by having a paid job alongside volunteer work in the sector you would like to move into. If you have no work at all and no immediate prospect of an income, you should look at unpaid opportunities but make sure that whoever is giving you that work is aware that if paid work were to come up, you would need to take it. It is always worth asking whether your employer will cover your travel and lunch costs to keep your outgoings to a minimum in unpaid or low-paid work. You should check with your local job centre for more information about how unpaid or volunteering work might impact upon any state benefits you are receiving.

'It is not how much experience you have; it is what you took from it that matters.'

Polishing up my experience stories

Work through the following list to ensure your experiences count

What are potential employers looking for from my experience?

....

....

....

....

....

....

Write a brief summary for two to three of my work-based experiences that demonstrate my skills and attributes.

....

....

....

....

....

....

....

....

List five experiences (personal or professional) that show skills that my preferred employers are looking for.

1 ....

2 ....

3 ....

4 ....

5 ....

Write a few examples of my skills and attributes demonstrated by my experiences.

....

....

....

....

....

Who will help me prepare to answer questions that interviewers might ask me about my work experience? When will I practise this?

....

....

....

....

....

What is my brand?

10 second summary

Your professional brand is a combination
of who you are (your skills, attributes
and experiences) and how you portray
yourself publicly.

Using my personal brand for professional success

Your professional brand will take some time to cultivate but will ultimately assist you in giving a good and clear impression of who you are, what you can do, and what your potential is. Having a brand will help potential employers to know what you are offering very quickly and easily, which boosts your chances of success.

By creating and maintaining your brand, you will also develop a very clear sense of what you can offer the job market and, therefore, what you want from that same market. It will also give you confidence when applying and interviewing for jobs.

'I didn't realise that everyone could see my personal photos online!'

My brand

Your brand is made up of all the public information there is about you, and employers are interested in it. You should take a moment to reflect on what information is already public and decide if it is the professional brand you would like to have. You can outsource the creation and maintenance of your online presence and brand but it will come with a cost, so decide if it is worth it first. For example, brandyourself.com, delightfulcommunications.com, and other companies will help you build your brand.

Brand Your professional identity as seen by potential employers. This could be through your professional website, your social media account, publications (online and print) that have involved you and your work, references, and online presence.

As with your career choice, your values and priorities will play a big part in your brand and you should avoid moving too far away from them.

Your brand has got to be truthful. However, it is sensible to look closely at what the companies you want to be part of are saying on their website and in their promotional material. If they are using key words that also align with your values and ambitions, then use them in your own brand. This makes it very easy for a potential employer to see how you would fit into their company.

Creating a professional brand

To create a professional brand, you need a clear understanding of what professional brands look like in your sector. You should also establish a good appreciation of what your current brand looks like and how you might want to alter it to match the expectations of your potential employers. Using the questions and directions below will help you to create a professional brand that suits you.

1   Research other people's professional brands – what speaks to you?

2   Ask a range of people in your network how they would describe you in three words and highlight the most common three that resonate with you.

3   Set up a website, a blog, a vlog, and an account on a professional networking platform such as LinkedIn (you may find specific ones depending on the field you are going into).

4   Include a picture of you looking professional on all platforms.

5   Using the three key words from step two, write a very brief description of yourself. (For example, 'Joe Bloggs: a diligent, creative team player'.)

6   After that, you should use your CV for inspiration and give a bit of background about yourself using full sentences and paragraphs. Try to avoid getting too wordy!

7   Make sure you include what it is you do (or want to do) and add your contact details to your platforms.

8   Put links to anything you have been involved in professionally such as articles, blogs, press statements, and so on.

9   Make sure your platforms are easy to find and include links at the bottom of your professional emails.

10   If you have not already, get a professional/neutral email address.

How do I promote my brand?

- Create and hand out business cards.

- Put your website at the bottom of emails.

- Go to networking events and conferences.

Once in a job, try to keep up with your online profile at least twice a year so that it remains relevant and accurate. You never know who might be looking at it and about to offer you a better job!

A student
told us

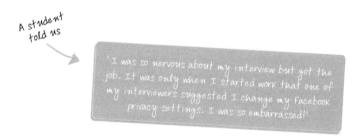

'I was so nervous about my interview but got the job. It was only when I started work that one of my interviewers suggested I change my Facebook privacy settings. I was so embarrassed!'

What should I do once I have my branded material ready?

Get someone who knows you well to check it. Do not put anything out into the public domain without someone proofreading it. It can be tempting to turn yourself into a perfectly packaged, successful entrepreneur in your branded material but if that is not who you are – or who you are likely to become any time soon – then it needs some revision. Your brand will change as you develop professionally but do not be tempted to create a dream version of yourself in the present.

Tip!

> Your brand reminds you of your professional self so be careful to create something you recognize and admire.

> 'Take control of your brand, take control of your future.'

CHECK POINT Promoting myself

Work through the following checklist

☐ I have reviewed what is already a part of my brand.

☐ I have reviewed my privacy settings.

☐ I have created my brand online using the following websites or platforms:

1 ....

2 ....

3 ....

4 ....

5 ....

☐ I have business cards (if appropriate).

☐ I have handed out my business cards or my contact details.

☐ I have drawn up my network.

☐ I have spread information about my brand through my network.

☐ I have a professional or neutral email address, which is:

....

Congratulations

You have now prepared for writing your CV, filling out applications, attending interviews, and have also established your brand.

Tick the boxes when you finish each section:

☐ Skills

☐ Attributes

☐ Experience

☐ Brand

How do I plan for success?

10 second summary

You can put a lot of effort into boosting your employability but without a clearly defined plan and achievable tasks, you might find success just out of reach.

Plan, prepare, and practise for career success

Life can feel very busy at times and so by fitting in defined tasks and deadlines, you will find that boosting your employability becomes much more manageable. You will know your timeframes the best and so make sure that you do not bite off more than you can chew. Make sure that each week you have added to your overall employability, rather than feeling disheartened that you did not complete all the tasks you set yourself.

Remember, this is not a sprint, it is a well-considered marathon and your success will rely on your planning and dedication.

Which planning method should I use?

Some methods include:

- to-do list

- flow chart

- gantt chart

- reminders on your computer/mobile/ tablet

- conversation with a mentor or manager (see below for more details about how to find a mentor)

> **Mentor** This is usually somebody in the job role you would like to be in. A mentor will give you information and guidance based on regular communication about your progress. You might find them in your workplace, through a professional body, or from a networking event.

I recommend that you avoid using a planning system that you need to spend a long time learning how to use; it is an excellent way to procrastinate and a terrible way to use your time effectively.

Finding a mentor

A mentor cannot be just anyone. You will need someone with a specific set of skills, attributes, and good availability. You should look for a mentor who has:

- a deep understanding of the sector you want to work in

- their own extensive network that could be used to benefit you

- the ability to reflect and action plan for themselves, as this can then be directed to help you

- good communication (particularly listening) skills

- the availability to dedicate the appropriate amount of time to you (This might be once a fortnight at the beginning, moving to once a month or once every few months as you grow more confident in what you are doing)

- excellent motivational skills

- the ability to respond to you reasonably quickly

- the skills that you need to develop so they can offer you clear guidance.

Motivation This is what drives you to do something and can be either intrinsic (from inside you) or extrinsic (external to you). For example, you may be intrinsically motivated by your intellectual curiosity to undertake an academic task or you may be extrinsically motivated by the grades you want to achieve.

You may find a mentor at work. In larger organizations, mentoring schemes are often in place, particularly for new members of staff. You should also check out any professional bodies that you are (or should be) registered with, as they tend to have a register of mentors or may be able to direct you to someone who could be of use. If you have neither of these options available to you, look to anyone in your network that ticks most of the above list and approach them.

Tip!

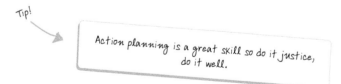

Action planning is a great skill so do it justice, do it well.

The time you spend in planning correlates to how successful and relaxed you are. A well-structured, clear, and detailed plan will save you hours of thinking about what to do next or how to do it. Your plan is a working document and will change to reflect your progress and your experiences.

ACTIVITY Planning for success

Have a look at the plan on the following page and make your own. Make sure that any action points that arise from the completion of a task get moved to become tasks themselves. It will be a positive reminder of how much you have achieved, so keep this document.

Be realistic about the amount of time you have to dedicate to boosting your employability. Avoid filling all your free time so it does not become a chore. Pinpoint a specific day and time to focus on your employability.

Tip!

At the end of each session, write a to-do list to help you get started for next time.

Task	Resources	Time allocated	Deadline	Review date	Action points
Write a CV	Online template, Super Quick Skills book on CVs: Write a Brilliant CV	3 hours	15th November	16th November with mum ✓	Get certificates in one envelope
Prepare a template covering letter	Online resources, template from careers advisor	1 hour	20th November	21st November with careers tutor ✓	
Identify five local companies I would like to work for	Business park website, walking around, asking friends and family	3 days	6th December	6th December with friend (AB)	
Get certifi-cates in one envelope		1 hour	27th November	27th November	

Who can help me?

You might choose to enlist the help of a careers advisor or personal tutor, a family member, or a friend. If you are seeking a promotion, it is advisable to ask your current manager or a colleague who is working at a higher level than you to assist you in setting relevant tasks.

Use your established network. They could take on many roles. See below a list of roles you may allocate to people in your network:

- time-keeper (keeping you to your deadlines)

- advisor in employability skills

- proofreader

- connector (helping you to expand your network)

- job-specific advisor (someone already in the job you want)

- motivator

- reflector (helps you to reflect and then plan)

- sounding board (to bounce ideas around with)

ACTIVITY Making my objectives SMART

Now that you have come this far in the book, have a go at writing yourself some SMART objectives.

....

....

....

....

....

....

....

....

....

....

....

....

....

....

....

....

....

'I feel a bit isolated and worried about keeping on top of setting and reviewing my objectives.'

'Be SMART about your objectives and you will succeed.'

How can I keep on track?

There are several ways you can do this:

- tick lists

- someone to check in with you regularly

- surrounding yourself with reminders and motivational quotations

Do not worry if you find that different things help you at different stages. This is to be expected, and it is a good habit to shake things up a bit to keep yourself feeling fresh and excited about the process of boosting your employability.

CHECK POINT Setting myself up to be SMART and successful

Work through the following list

☐ I have made a plan.

☐ I have set SMART objectives.

☐ I have contacted people from my network for support. Their names are:

....

....

....

☐ I have a measure for success in place.

☐ I have ways to ensure I stay on track. They are:

....

....

....

....

....

....

How do I activate my plan?

10 second summary

Having a plan is one thing, beginning to get to grips with it is another. Reading this section will help if you are struggling to know when, where, or how to start activating your plan.

**Finding your starting point, keeping on track, reaching the
finishing line**

Having a gorgeous plan is clearly not enough, you need to then activate the
plan to achieve your objectives. It can be a daunting process for anyone
and knowing when, where, and how to begin will give you the confidence
to get started and to keep going. This section will inspire you to set your
plan into motion with a sense of calm determination and you will feel a lot
better once it is started.

Action planning is a skill that is transferable to many areas in work and
life. Learning what works best for you now will be endlessly helpful to
you in the future.

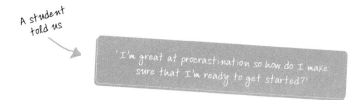

'I'm great at procrastination so how do I make
sure that I'm ready to get started?'

Preparing to start

Choose a day and time when you know you will have space and peace to focus wholly on the tasks ahead.

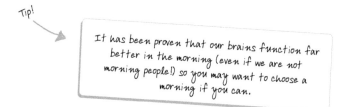

Tip!

It has been proven that our brains function far better in the morning (even if we are not morning people!) so you may want to choose a morning if you can.

It is a good idea to think in advance about what you will need to have in place (particularly if you want to talk with someone and need to make an appointment), where you will be (is the space clear and ready for you to fill it with your project?), what time you will get started (make that appointment with yourself and keep it so that you do not become distracted), and how long you will dedicate to the tasks (a time frame always inspires productivity).

Have the following things nearby:

- motivational quotes and/or pictures

- a snack and drink to keep energised

- a treat planned (chocolate, a book to read, a game to play, a person to call)

- pen and paper

> 'A task always seems bigger in anticipation.'

For the initial session, I would recommend no longer than an hour. This will be sufficient to give you a good start at your tasks but not so long that you become weary of them. Ideally, you want each session to be long enough to achieve one to five tasks (depending on the size of the task). You certainly do not want to become bored or tired through the session and you really should aim to finish each session feeling excited about your next one.

Tip!

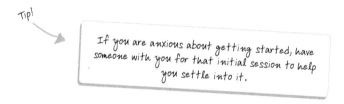

If you are anxious about getting started, have someone with you for that initial session to help you settle into it.

What if something goes wrong?

It is almost inevitable that something (usually minor) goes awry; your plan is a working document and you should feel free to alter it as you go along. If you thought that someone would be able to assist you in a task and then they are not available, the fix is easy: choose a different person or change the time frame for the task. If you get part way through your job search and realize that you have changed your mind about what you want to do, then take this as a positive; it shows you have developed your ideas through the process.

If something does not go as expected, give yourself some time to reflect on what happened so that it does not happen again. If you feel disheartened, arrange to speak with someone in your network who will be able to listen to how you feel, help you pick out the positives, and motivate you again.

'A wrong path helps us to recognize the right one.'

Be flexible

I have already suggested that you have a detailed plan to begin with. As you go along you may find it needs flexibility built in with regard to timing, task order, deadlines, and who will be involved. You will get a feel of your plan and the correct level of flexibility as you go along.

CHECK POINT Activating the plan

Fill out the below to help you get started

When will you begin tackling your plan?

....

....

Where will you be when you do this?

....

....

What do you need in preparation for it?

....

....

....

How long are you are allocating yourself?

....

....

Which tasks will you undertake in this first session?

....

....

....

Congratulations

You have activated your plan for success!

Write down three positive words about how you feel about your plan:

1 ....

2 ....

3 ....

What are my next steps?

10 second
summary

You could reflect on your career and create action plans at any stage. It is useful for you to know *how* to reflect and plan at each stage in a way that serves you best.

Reflect on your journey and plan the path ahead

Reflection is a useful process to ensure that you are on track and that you are still getting the most out of your job. Reflection should always lead to an action plan. Reflection is a chance for you to celebrate your successes, analyse your experiences, and plan for development.

There are many ways to reflect, and what suits you may differ from what suits your colleagues, your manager, your friends. Your workplace is likely to offer you a regular review meeting. Self-reflection and action planning before this meeting will help prepare you to make the most of it.

A student told us

'I've heard about reflecting and action planning from my manager but I don't know what I should do!'

When should I reflect on my career?

- At the outset of your new career (within three months).

- Every three to four months.

- Once a year make time for an overview reflection and planning moment (possibly at work).

What method of reflection might I use?

There are multiple methods of reflection and finding one that suits you is important. Methods include:

- Taking pictures of the things you have done well/need to improve on and collecting them together on a board.

- Keeping a log of your Continuous Professional Development (CPD).

CPD (Continuous Professional Development) This is about what you will be doing in terms of formal and informal training and development. This could include attending a training course, having a professional discussion with a colleague, observing/shadowing another professional, self-reflection, gathering feedback on your performance, and creating an action plan.

- Keeping a computer file with key documents that show your achievements and a running list of things to do.

- Using a SWOT analysis (Strengths, Weaknesses, Opportunities, Threats).

- Using the Professional Development Review (PDR) format used by your workplace.

- Having a chat with a mentor (internal or external to your organization).

There are too many to list them all here and you could research other methods online if the above do not work for you.

SWOT analysis This is a self-reflection tool that will help you to create an action plan. Dividing a piece of paper into four quarters, label the sections with the following: strengths, weaknesses, opportunities, and threats. Under 'strengths', list the things that you have in place to help you succeed. Beneath 'weaknesses', list the areas of your own performance that you would need to develop. Under 'opportunities', list all the opportunities and resources you have to help you achieve, such as people, courses, materials, and so on. Under 'threats', list all the things that might become obstacles to your success.

PDR (Professional Development Review) This is a regular opportunity to discuss your progress, skills development, success, and areas for development with your manager. It is a chance to review and set targets. You should receive a written record of this meeting.

Should someone else be involved in my reflection?

A mentor, a friend, a colleague, a manager, an ex-colleague, or a relative could be useful to you in the reflection process. Professional bodies quite often have a mentoring system in place that you could take up if you felt this would be most useful to you.

Tip!

If you feel that the reflection session did not work for you (it did not result in a clear action plan or make you feel motivated) then change the way you are doing it.

What if I feel negatively about my job?

Most career journeys will have peaks and troughs so try to take a step back and see your career in its entirety. Reflect on the past year in your job and try to pinpoint what is making you feel negatively about it. Once you have identified the issue, look forward and try to establish whether the problem will go away on its own or whether you need a plan in place to change it.

Tip!

Talking about your negative feelings to a colleague can be unhelpful as they may be a reminder of those feelings going forward.

Getting and using feedback

I would recommend that you always ask for feedback in a professional and formal/semi-formal manner as you are asking someone to take time to think about your performance. The person giving feedback may find it useful for you to give them up to three specific things you want feedback on.

'Feedback is a gift.'

The 360-degree review model includes feedback from your manager, a peer, someone who works beneath you, and your own reflections.

Your reflections based on feedback should feed into your action plan, focusing on areas that you have identified as ripe for development. You should use all of this when having your Professional Development Review (or equivalent) with your manager.

'Reflect on the past, plan for the future.'

ACTIVITY Motivation

It is useful to first establish what your motivations are. Some examples are listed below; feel free to add your own to the list.

Intrinsic (internal to you)	Extrinsic (external to you/from others)
• pride	• money
• curiosity	• status
• interest	• recognition from others
• passion	• instant gratification
•	•
•	•
•	•

Tip!

If involving someone else, check that they have enough time to contribute to you and your plan. You will find it frustrating if your progress is held up by someone else.

ACTIVITY Reflection time

Plan an hour when you can spend some time reflecting on your work experience. If you are going to chat with a mentor, book a time with them and plan what you want to raise in the conversation (achievements, concerns, plans).

Once you have reflected, record the key points so you can review them at your next reflection opportunity.

....

....

....

....

....

....

....

....

....

....

....

....

....

....

....

....

Limit the time that you spend on boosting your employability, allowing for an amount of time that will reasonably fit into your life.

If you choose to take time off, set yourself a specific date when you will return to the subject so that you can truly relax, knowing that you will go back to it.

CHECK POINT — Keeping on going!

Work through the following questions to ensure you keep up the momentum

How regularly will I update my CV?

....

....

When will I monitor my brand materials?

....

....

What training opportunities am I looking for (in-house and externally)?

....

....

How and when will I get in touch with my network?

....

....

How will I keep an eye on opportunities for promotion or career progression through changing employers?

....

....

Final checklist: How to know you are done

Use this checklist to make sure that you have completed each section.

Are your aims and SMART objectives planned? ☐

Is your network established? ☐

Do you have a recognized professional self? ☐

Have you carried out research on companies and
organizations that are of interest? ☐

Are your job priorities set? ☐

Have you considered, written down, and prepared
your skills, attributes, and experiences for interview? ☐

Have you started your action plan? ☐

Have you reflected on feedback? ☐

Have you planned your next steps and
begun work on your new objectives? ☐

Glossary

Aim A broad view of what you would like to achieve. This could be short-term (a few days or weeks), mid-term (a few months) or long-term (a year or more). It should be broken down into and supported by SMART objectives. The aim is the overview of your objectives.

Attributes These are your personal qualities that can be polished but are unlikely to change dramatically. They are things such as honesty, personal presentation, positive attitude, reliability, self-management, enthusiasm, social responsibility and autonomy.

Brand Your professional identity as seen by potential employers. This could be through your professional website, your social media account, publications (online and print) that have involved you and your work, references, and online presence.

CPD (Continuous Professional Development) This is about what you will be doing in terms of formal and informal training and development. This could include attending a training course, having a professional discussion with a colleague, observing/shadowing another professional, self-reflection, gathering feedback on your performance, and creating an action plan.

CV (Curriculum Vitae) A document outlining your attributes, skills, work experience, and achievements. This should be no longer than two A4 pages and should include your contact details. Your CV is to be submitted to potential employers as a brief explanation of who you are and what you can do. Potential employers will decide whether to offer you an interview based on this.

Employability The things that make you employable such as skills, attributes, and experience. The presentation of this information about you is important to your overall success in becoming employed.

Graduate attributes These are attributes that are usually associated with graduates as they tend to relate to academia. They might include intellectual curiosity, research presentation, critical thinking, problem solving, communication skills, creativity, and so on.

Hidden job market This describes all the jobs that are not being advertised publicly but are being shown on individual company websites, internal to an organization or through word-of-mouth. For example, a manager may ask their team to put forward anyone they know who might be interested in the job vacancy. This is where your networking will be useful.

Mentor This is usually somebody in the job role you would like to be in. A mentor will give you information and guidance based on regular communication about your progress. You might find them in your workplace, through a professional body, or from a networking event.

Motivation This is what drives you to do something and can be either intrinsic (from inside you) or extrinsic (external to you). For example, you may be intrinsically motivated by your intellectual curiosity to undertake an academic task or you may be extrinsically motivated by the grades you want to achieve.

Network This is a group of people who you can speak with about your career. A network can include relatives, friends, ex-colleagues, current colleagues, managers, teachers, academic supervisors, professional mentors, and people in the same field of work who might be able to help you.

Objectives These should be SMART and should all work together to achieve your overall aim. They can be small individual objectives or interconnected objectives, each relying on the completion of others. These can be short-term, mid-term or long-term.

PDR (Professional Development Review) This is a regular opportunity to discuss your progress, skills development, success, and areas for development with your manager. It is a chance to review and set targets. You should receive a written record of this meeting.

Skills These are things you have had to learn or develop, either formally or informally. They include project management, organizational skills, stress management, time management, communication skills, leadership skills, and flexibility. This could also include more job-specific areas such as accountancy, computer skills, teaching skills, and so on.

SMART   This relates to the objectives you set yourself, which should be specific, measurable, attainable, relevant and time-based. An objective needs to be all these things so that you can achieve it.

SWOT analysis   This is a self-reflection tool that will help you to create an action plan. Dividing a piece of paper into four quarters, label the sections with the following: strengths, weaknesses, opportunities, and threats. Under 'strengths', list the things that you have in place to help you succeed. Beneath 'weaknesses', list the areas of your own performance that you would need to develop. Under 'opportunities', list all the opportunities and resources you have to help you achieve, such as people, courses, materials, and so on. Under 'threats', list all the things that might become obstacles to your success.

Values   These are the core things that you hold dear such as honesty, maintaining a work-life balance, family, and so on. If these differ from the values of the company you work for, you may find this a difficult situation to be in.

Work experience   This could be from paid or unpaid work and includes any experience in which you were responsible for performing tasks to achieve a set goal for the benefit of a work project or work team.

Further reading and resources

Check out other books in the Super Quick Skills series such as:

Becker, L. (2020) *Write a Brilliant CV.* London: Sage

Becker, L. (2020) *Give Great Presentations.* London: Sage

Check out my other book on career success:

Becker, L. & Becker, F. (2016) *Seven Steps to a Successful Career.* London: Sage

The following website is a useful website to go to for information on your employment rights:

www.gov.uk

The following websites can help you develop your professional brand:

www.linkedin.com

www.glassdoor.co.uk

www.brandyourself.com

www.delightfulcommunications.com

Milton Keynes UK
Ingram Content Group UK Ltd.
UKHW050640031224
3319UKWH00068B/828

9 781529 745009